Sundays
on the
Go

90 Seconds
with the Weekly Gospel

Sundays
on the
Go

YEAR A

ALBERT HAASE, OFM

PARACLETE PRESS
Brewster, Massachusetts

2022 First Printing

Sundays on the Go: 90 Seconds with Sunday's Gospel, Year A

Copyright © 2022 by Franciscan Friars of the State of Missouri

ISBN 978-1-64060-825-2

The Paraclete Press name and logo are trademarks of Paraclete Press.

Library of Congress Cataloging-in-Publication Data
Names: Haase, Albert, 1955- author.
Title: Sundays on the go : 90 seconds with Sunday's gospel, year A / Albert
   Haase, OFM.
Description: Brewster, Massachusetts : Paraclete Press, 2022. | Summary: "A
   short reflection, a prayer, and a question to ponder for each Sunday's
   Gospel through the year"-- Provided by publisher.
Identifiers: LCCN 2022021717 | ISBN 9781640608252 | ISBN 9781640608269
   (epub) | ISBN 9781640608276 (pdf)
Subjects: LCSH: Bible. Gospels--Devotional literature. | Church
   year--Prayers and devotions. | Common lectionary (1992). Year A.
Classification: LCC BS2555.54 .H33 2022 | DDC 252/.6--dc23/eng/20220622
LC record available at https://lccn.loc.gov/2022021717

10 9 8 7 6 5 4 3 2 1

Published by Paraclete Press
Brewster, Massachusetts
www.paracletepress.com

Printed in the United States of America

In memory of Thomas Vos, OFM,
who showed me the Gospel's light by the
way he lived with blindness.

CONTENTS

LENT

HOLY WEEK

THE EASTER SEASON

ORDINARY TIME

SOLEMNITIES AND SPECIAL FEASTS

INTRODUCTION

My first assignment as a newly ordained priest was being a pastoral staff member at St. Peter's Church in Chicago's business district commonly called "the Loop." In the early '80s, it was a hub of spiritual activity, with fourteen daily Masses and confessions from 6:30 a.m. to 7:00 p.m.

With so many daily Masses that virtually doubled on Holy Days of Obligation, the presider was always challenged to keep the homily short and sweet. Thanks to that first year of ministry, I developed the habit of preaching brief, and hopefully direct, daily homilies.

"Father Albert," Valerie recently told me, "I love catching Jesus on the run with you. Why don't you write your pithy homilies into a book?"

Sundays on the Go: 90 Seconds with Sunday's Gospel, Year A, is offered in that spirit. It contains a short reflection, prayer, and reflection question for each Sunday's Gospel. I have deliberately limited myself to 170–180 words. Though occasionally offering comments on the meaning of the feast, most of the reflections focus on the Gospel.

In preparation for attending the Sunday Eucharist, I invite you to read the Gospel. Then read the reflection and the prayer, and conclude with the reflection question. That question can be used during the week to help you stay in touch with Sunday's Gospel.

As we journey together during Year A of the liturgical cycle, I hope we all are blessed by meeting Jesus on the go.

Albert Haase, OFM
Sunday of the Word of God

Sundays
on the
Go

 *ADVENT*

A Cure for Sleepwalkers

Advent is a time for us to look back and ponder an incredible love story that blossomed two thousand years ago in the insignificant, small town of Bethlehem—yet our Gospel invites us to live in the present as we anticipate the future. Just as the flood in Noah's time caught people off guard and unaware, so too Christ's Second Coming will come unannounced and catch people unprepared. Rather than go through our day as sleepwalkers doing everything by rote and routine, we are challenged this Advent to "stay awake!" As a Poor Clare nun once told me, "Christ comes in disguise and as a surprise— and never makes an appointment!"

Pray

Jesus,
You took flesh in a stable two thousand years ago and will come again. Don't let us be content to live with the old, sentimental memories of a manger and your Virgin Mother.

Sharpen our senses and make us mindful of the myriad manifestations of your majesty in this moment. Amen.

Ponder

What spiritual practices awaken me from my spiritual slumber?

Become a Construction Worker

When dignitaries traveled in the ancient world, they would send workers ahead to fill in potholes and level the bumpy parts of the road. This ensured their chariots and carriages would travel along smoothly and without consequence. Today's Gospel associates Isaiah's prophecy with John the Baptist: "A voice of one crying out in the desert, Prepare the way of the Lord, make straight his paths." John makes it clear that we are called to fill in the potholes in our lives and make the road for the coming dignitary straight by repenting of our sins and doing good deeds. We don't want him to detour. It's easy to forget that Advent assumes repentance.

Pray

Jesus,

The Baptist challenges us to prepare for your coming. May we live with such integrity and good deeds that you will find the roads in our lives and to our hearts smooth.

May we do nothing to hinder you on your journey. Amen.

Ponder

What potholes in my life need to be filled in? What roads need to be leveled?

THIRD SUNDAY OF ADVENT
(MATTHEW 11:2–11)

Talk Is Cheap

When John's disciples asked Jesus if he was the longed-for Messiah, he surprisingly didn't reply with a resounding "Yes!" Rather, he replied with the marvels and miracles of his ministry: "The blind regain their sight, the lame walk, lepers are cleansed, the deaf hear, the dead are raised, and the poor have the good news proclaimed to them." Jesus was only too aware that actions speak louder than words. Perhaps we are too quick to reply in the affirmative when asked if we are Christians or believe in God. Better for us to follow Jesus's lead and let our thoughts and actions speak for themselves; they will bolster or betray our words.

THIRD SUNDAY OF ADVENT

Pray

Jesus,

You call us to imitate you in our witness to your Father's dream for all creation.

May our proclamation of the kingdom of God go beyond mere words and become incarnate in our actions.

May our lives be an announcement of your coming in our midst.

Amen.

Ponder

How do my thoughts and actions bolster or betray my belief in Christ's coming among us?

No Talk, All Action

At Brother Jerome's funeral, a Franciscan friar paid the deceased one of the highest compliments I've ever heard. "Brother Jerome was a man of few words. He had the uncanny ability to know what God wanted him to do and he did it without complaint or fanfare." The same can be said of Saint Joseph. He never utters a word in the Gospels. He emerges as an obedient man who discerns God's will and obeys it without a question or a doubt. He is a living incarnation of what Advent calls each one of us to have: an awakened, discerning heart that instantly responds with action.

Pray

Saint Joseph,
Unlike Mary who proclaimed, "Let it be done to me as you say," you have left us no words of wisdom by which to live our lives.

You only have left us your example of heroic obedience despite the precarious situation in which you found yourself.

Like you, may we be awake and follow God's commands.

Amen.

Ponder

When have I hesitated or refused to respond to the call of God?

The Good, the Bad,
and the Ugly

Like many twenty-first-century people, the author of the Gospel of Matthew had an interest in genealogy. We can only shake our heads in disbelief as he mentions people with spotty reputations in Jesus's ancestry. There is mention of a murderer and adulterer (David), a prostitute (Rahab), a woman who pretended to be a prostitute (Tamar), a sexually forward widow (Ruth), and a woman taken in adultery (Bathsheba). Why not obliterate the memories of such people to preserve Jesus's dignity and divinity? Perhaps Matthew wanted to highlight that Jesus is truly human—one just like us—who has shady relatives with skeletons in their closets.

Pray

Jesus,

Your ancestors had flaws, weaknesses, and sins. And yet, you not only accepted their bloodline and DNA, but you heartily embraced it.

In doing so, you manifested the Father's unconditional love not in spite of our sin, but with our sin.

By embracing our humanity, you offer us a path to share in your divinity.

Amen.

Ponder

What relatives of mine do I hesitate to embrace because of their perceived sinfulness?

The Wonder of Weakness

Like parents remembering the arrival of each of their children, we know the details of Christmas only too well: a census, a trip to Bethlehem, a woman pregnant with her firstborn, an inn with no vacancy, a manger, swaddling clothes, shepherds keeping night watch, angels in the sky, "Glory to God in the highest and on earth peace to those on whom his favor rests." What sometimes gets lost in the details is a stunning surprise: the Lord and King of the Universe's humility, fragility, and utter dependence on two parents. This king inspires wonder by walking the way of weakness.

Pray

Jesus,
You did not come to us in splendor and grandeur, riding the clouds of glory. Perhaps you knew this might instill in us fear and dread. Instead, you came to us as a baby who needed to be nursed, changed, and taught.

May your weakness inspire us to embrace our own fragility and dependence on your Father.

Amen.

Ponder

How does the birth of Jesus challenge me to embrace the weakness of my own humanity?

The "Thing" of Christmas

Unlike German, a precise language with a specific word for just about anything and everything, Chinese sometimes struggles for a precise word. The common word *shìqíng* ("thing"), is a case in point: it can refer to a situation, business, affair, or matter. It's used in the translation of the shepherds' statement, "Let us go, then, to Bethlehem to see this thing that has taken place, which the Lord has made known to us." The word trips, falters, and deflates before the stupendous mystery of God taking on human flesh. It subtly reminds us that the ineffable event of Christmas challenges the constraints of any human language.

Pray

Father,

The mystery of the Incarnation baffles us.

How can we understand or comprehend the love, creativity, and ingenuity it portrays?

As we kneel before the manger of Bethlehem, may we live with the awareness that the only adequate description of this event is the silence of wonder and awe.

Amen.

Ponder

How would I describe the meaning of Christmas to an alien from another planet?

The Word Became a Pilgrim

It's one of the most famous sentences from John's Gospel and an excellent description of today's feast: "And the Word became flesh and made his dwelling among us." In a culture where people brought their tents with them when traveling, the literal translation of the original Greek states the message of Christmas bluntly and concretely, ". . . and pitched his tent among us." Not only did the Eternal Word of the Father embrace our human flesh, but he also cast his lot with us and embraced the precariousness of our pilgrim way of life.

THE NATIVITY OF THE LORD, MASS DURING THE DAY

Pray

Jesus,

By journeying to Bethlehem and pitching your tent among us, you have joined us on the pilgrimage of life.

As we experience the inconveniences of traveling with changing weather conditions, may we look to you as our guide and follow your footprints off the beaten path of this world's understanding of success and happiness.

May the journey lead us to our eternal home.

Amen.

Ponder

How has my life been a pilgrimage? Where am I headed?

Life and Death

Filled stockings hung on the mantel. A lit Christmas tree with wrapped presents beneath it. A battery-powered Santa Claus that says, "Ho, ho, ho! Merry Christmas!" Cookies and milk by the fireplace. The song "Rudolph the Red-Nosed Reindeer." It's so easy to associate the celebration of Christmas with children. Today's feast, however, contrasts starkly with yesterday's feast and reminds us that Christmas calls for an adult commitment. The Gospel reminds us that the splendor of the crib is shrouded with the shadow of the cross. Life and death walk hand-in-hand in the Christian experience. The birth of Jesus leads to the death of Saint Stephen, and the martyr's death leads to birth into eternal glory.

FEAST OF SAINT STEPHEN, FIRST MARTYR

Pray

Saint Stephen,
You proclaimed the gospel not only with your words but also with your very life.

May your death instill in us a constant fidelity to our baptismal promises.

May we be inspired to take seriously our commitment to the Babe of Bethlehem.

Amen.

Ponder

What are practical ways that I can live out my adult commitment to the Christ Child?

The Gift of Friendship

Though biblical scholars doubt that the "other disciple whom Jesus loved" mentioned in today's Gospel is the same person as John the apostle and evangelist, tradition has linked them together as the same person. This disciple's description as being loved by Jesus celebrates a unique friendship and intimacy between the two. At the Last Supper, this disciple reclined in the place of honor, immediately next to Jesus. He followed the arrested Jesus to the courtyard of Annas the high priest. He is the only male who stood at the foot of the cross. On entering the empty tomb, he "saw and believed." Jesus was blessed to have such a faithful friend.

FEAST OF SAINT JOHN, APOSTLE AND EVANGELIST

Pray

Saint John, beloved by Jesus,
You are a wonderful example of loyalty in friendship.

You were neither embarrassed to follow Jesus as he was arrested nor afraid to stand beneath the cross.

You were the first to believe in the resurrection of your friend.

May we be given the gift of being such friends to others.

Amen.

Ponder

How do I treat the friends God has given me?

Unrestrained Hungers of the Heart

Today's Gospel portrays a power-hungry Herod who decided to destroy any future competition that could potentially threaten his authority and control of the people. Herod's lust for power is as appalling and tragic as the deaths of the Holy Innocents. This Gospel challenges us to take a hard, honest look at ourselves and ask what the hungers, cravings, and obsessions are for which we are willing to slaughter the reputation, career, or potential of another. It is so easy to victimize others for the sake of our pride, our position in the office, or our need to bask alone in the prestige or publicity of the moment.

Pray

Jesus,

Your birth as the Prince of Peace threatened Herod and made him respond with violence.

His decision to murder the two-year-old boys in Bethlehem and its vicinity betrays an obsession that has gotten out of control.

May we live with self-awareness and keep our hungers and cravings in check.

Amen.

Ponder

What are the hungers, cravings, and obsessions for which I am willing to slaughter another person's reputation, career, or potential?

THE HOLY FAMILY OF JESUS, MARY, AND JOSEPH
(MATTHEW 2:13–15, 19–23)

There's No Place Like Home

Like contemporary refugees, the Holy Family kept on the move: first to Egypt, then to Israel, then to the region of Galilee, and finally making a home in Nazareth. A family is looking for protection; a family is looking for a home. Becoming a family and making a home just don't happen—they are adventures that need to be intentionally and enthusiastically embraced. Becoming a family requires relationships that call forth, celebrate, and offer opportunities to put God-given gifts to use. Making a home involves providing a safe place to fall, where everyone feels sheltered, loved, and nourished. Family and home can become the wombs of saints.

THE HOLY FAMILY OF JESUS, MARY, AND JOSEPH

Pray

Mary, Joseph, and Jesus,
Your early life together reveals the
challenges and inconveniences of
becoming a family and making a home.

You stayed together and embraced
those trials without hesitation.

May your example inspire us when
hardships and troubles threaten our
families.

May our families and our home life
help us grow in holiness.

Amen.

Ponder

What are the typical challenges and
inconveniences that threaten my family
and home?

Touched by God

John's Gospel begins with the very same words as the Book of Genesis, "In the beginning." In Genesis, these words are time sensitive and note the moment of the creation of the heavens and the earth; in the Fourth Gospel, they push back even farther to the eternal existence of God. The Word was God and always abided with God. This Word, through whom "all things came to be," was the mold around which everything was created; it was like a sieve through which every created thing passed. "Without [the Word] nothing came to be." All creation—from hail to a hippopotamus to a human—has been affected by the Word made flesh. Everything has been touched by God.

Pray

Word made flesh,
Your imprint shimmers and shines in
creation.

Because everything has been shaped
by you, in you, and through you, every
created thing becomes a ladder to you.

May we climb this ladder and be filled
with wonder and awe over the myriad
expressions of your divine creativity.

Amen.

Ponder

How have I been shaped by the Word?

The Gospel of the Stable's Animals

The animals in the stable at Bethlehem tell us a lot about the meaning of today's feast. There is the donkey that Mary, pregnant with Jesus, rode on. This beast of burden is not known for its intelligence. There are sheep, brought there by the shepherds. Sheep are known to be dirty and smelly. And there are the magi's three camels with the odd-looking hump on their backs. These animals proclaim their own unique gospel: if there is room in that stable, around that manger, for an unintelligent donkey, stinky sheep, and odd-looking camels, there is room in there for you and me. Jesus is the savior for all: Jew and Gentile, intelligent and ignorant, flawless and filthy, handsome and homely.

Pray

Jesus,
You did not come to us just as a
redeemer for the chosen few.

You came for women and men of every
race, color, gender, and religion.

May we never hesitate to kneel in your
presence.

Amen.

Ponder

What do I think makes me unworthy
to be in the presence of the Christ Child?

To Fulfill All Righteousness

Only in Matthew's Gospel do Jesus and John discuss Jesus's baptism. Jesus tells an unwilling John to baptize him, "for thus it is fitting for us to fulfill all righteousness." The word *righteousness*, appearing seven times in Matthew's Gospel, sounds peculiar to our contemporary ears. It was applied earlier to Joseph and later will be applied to Jesus's disciples in the Sermon on the Mount. It suggests a right relationship with God, others, oneself, and all creation; it is accomplished through fidelity to the demands of God's covenant. Baptism is not only our immersion into the death and resurrection of Jesus but also our commitment to faithfully live in alignment with the kingdom of God's relationships.

Pray

Jesus,

Though you had no need of John's baptism of repentance, you willingly gave yourself over to it.

In doing so, you gave us an example of humility and submission.

May our thoughts, words, and actions always submit and be aligned to the primary relationships of the kingdom of God.

Amen.

Ponder

How do my baptismal promises find expression in my primary relationships?

 LENT

Reboot Your Spiritual Life

Today begins the forty days of Lent. It is a sacred time of reflection and penance. It also offers us the opportunity to reboot our spiritual lives. In today's Gospel, Jesus offers us a trinity of ancient practices that not only does that but also strengthens the three important relationships in our lives. Prayer brings us in communion with God. Fasting challenges us to look at our bodies and our lifestyles and ask how we regard them. Alms giving moves our attention away from ourselves to our neighbor. Each spiritual practice can transform a hardened heart into a fiery furnace of fidelity.

Pray

Spirit of the Living God,
Give us the grace of a prayer life that
intensifies our love for you.

Help us to fast from the distractions
and diversions that offer a false sense of
satisfaction and security.

Break open our hearts in charitable acts of
generosity.

May all our Lenten practices set us on fire
with peace, love, and justice.

Amen.

Ponder

How will I practice prayer, fasting, and
alms giving during this Lenten season?

Will I Be Faithful?

As preparation for his ministry, Jesus was led by the Spirit into the desert. He fasted for forty days and forty nights, and afterward, in that moment of vulnerability, the devil made his move to test Jesus. Jesus is reliving the period of testing experienced by his people when they wandered for forty years in the wilderness of Sinai. There God scrutinized the chosen people to see whether they would remain faithful to the covenant. While Israel proved unfaithful by grumbling against Moses and testing God, Jesus remained staunchly faithful to his relationship with God and his identity as the Beloved Son. Ultimately, this Gospel presents the challenge of all testing by the devil: will we remain faithful to our relationship with the Father and our identity as the children of God? The decision is ours.

Pray

Jesus,

As the forty days of Lent continue, we are reminded of the power of evil in our lives.

May we have the insight to uncover and renounce any temptation that we face.

Amen.

Ponder

What strengthens me in moments of temptation?

Mystical Moments

Matthew's description of the Transfiguration suggests a mystical moment witnessed by Peter, James, and John. Jesus's face shines like the sun; his clothes become white as light; Moses, representing the Law, and Elijah, representing the prophets, appear and converse with him. There is the shadow cast by a bright cloud with a voice coming from that cloud that proclaims Jesus as the beloved Son. Like many of us in times of intense and gratifying prayer, Peter wants to capture the moment and freeze it. But that is not meant to happen. Mystical moments such as the Transfiguration are gifts and graces that God occasionally offers us to spiritually invigorate us. They are meant to be pondered—"listen to him"—and, as

Jesus charged the disciples not to speak of what happened, they are not necessarily to be shared with others.

———

Pray

Loving God,
You sometimes grace our prayer with mystical moments similar to the Transfiguration.

May such moments move us to listen more deeply to your Son and follow him more closely.

Amen.

Ponder

When have I experienced intense and gratifying periods of prayer?

Bring Your Bucket to Jesus

Jesus's encounter with the woman at the well happened "about noon," the hottest part of the day. Consequently, it was only natural that their conversation should center around thirst and water. It's clear Jesus and the woman are miscommunicating since Jesus is speaking of a spiritual water that permanently slakes our thirst while the woman is speaking of everyday water that we need to drink time and again. The woman's continued thirst is evident in the many husbands she has had—and her current live-in boyfriend. How tempting it is to look beyond ourselves in hopes that people, possessions, prestige, or popularity will slake the thirst of our souls. Only Jesus provides "a spring of water welling up to eternal life" that slakes our thirst forever.

Pray

Jesus,

In your teaching and life, you provide us with the spring of living water that slakes our thirst.

May we never look beyond ourselves for satisfaction.

May we discover within ourselves the spring of eternal life.

Amen.

Ponder

When do I look beyond myself for the fulfillment of my deepest desires?

In Need of an Optometrist?

When asked if there was anything worse than physical blindness, Helen Keller famously quipped, "Yes! Having no vision." In today's Gospel, the man born blind was healed of his disability by Jesus. But it wasn't just a physical healing. As the story progresses, we see the healed man's spiritual vision sharpen. He first referred to Jesus as "the man called Jesus." A little later, he called Jesus "a prophet." And then, at the end of today's passage, he called Jesus "Lord" and worshiped him. If we can read this reflection, we have our eyesight. But just because we have our eyesight doesn't mean we have the 20/20 vision that the healed man gradually came to in today's Gospel. Our thoughts, words, and actions tell us whether we need to visit a spiritual optometrist.

FOURTH SUNDAY OF LENT

Pray

Jesus,

Like the man in today's Gospel, we too are born blind—often to our weaknesses and sins.

Give us sight.

Sharpen our spiritual vision so we can proclaim you as Lord of our lives.

Amen.

Ponder

How does my spiritual vision affect my life?

From Tomb to Womb

Given the Jewish belief that a deceased person's spirit hovered around the corpse for three days, Martha's comment to Jesus's order to take the tomb's stone door away highlights the utter hopelessness of the moment: "Lord, by now there will be a stench; he has been dead for four days." But "the glory of God" incarnated in Jesus who is "the resurrection and the life" cannot be defeated or outdone in the Fourth Gospel. The raising of Lazarus is the defining moment of Jesus's public ministry and reminds us that no situation is too definitive or impervious to God's grace and action. Even death must give way to divine love. Jesus comes, stands before the tombs of our lives and, calling our names, transforms them into wombs of hope and new life.

Pray

Jesus,
Our belief in you gives us hope in the face of devastating disappointments and traumatic tragedies.

May we never doubt your presence and love in our lives.

Amen.

Ponder

When did God transform a tomb into a womb of hope for me?

HOLY WEEK

A New Age Has Dawned

Immediately after the death of Jesus, Matthew adds a detail not found in the other Gospels: "The earth quaked, rocks were split, tombs were opened, and the bodies of many saints who had fallen asleep were raised. And coming forth from their tombs after his resurrection, they entered the holy city and appeared to many." In an earlier passage, Jesus had predicted that earthquakes would accompany the "labor pains" that signify the birth of a new age. This new age of resurrection, prophesied by Ezekiel's vision of the dry bones coming to life and rising from their graves, and by Daniel's vision of the just rising to everlasting life, has now broken in. Jesus's death begins a new age where death no longer has the final word.

Pray

Jesus,

Your death provides the portal to a world we never thought imaginable.

Death is no longer a definitive end. It is the birth canal to new life, to an eternal life.

May this knowledge be a source of our hope.

Amen.

Ponder

How will I journey with Jesus this Holy Week?

Humility and Love

In John's description of the Last Supper, Jesus did not offer bread and wine as his body and blood to his disciples. Instead, he washed the feet of his disciples, a chore only done by the lowliest servants of the household. This act of kneeling and pouring water over the disciples' feet foreshadowed the upcoming act of humility as Jesus fell to his knees, embraced the cross, and poured out his blood. Both acts of humility were done out of love. Jesus reminded his disciples that such humble love formed the model of behavior for all who have bathed in the waters of Baptism and follow him as "teacher and master."

Pray

Loving Jesus,
The final days of your life highlighted your entire ministry of humility and love.

By emptying yourself in humility by washing feet and embracing the cross, you showed us the meaning of selfless love.

May our lives of humble love witness to our bath in the waters of Baptism.

Amen.

Ponder

In what practical ways do I live humility and love?

GOOD FRIDAY
(JOHN 18:1–19:42)

Were You There When They Crucified My Lord?

In today's Gospel, Judas accompanied the soldiers and guards who arrested Jesus. Standing around a charcoal fire, Simon Peter denied Jesus three times. Though finding no guilt in Jesus, Pilate was frightened, threatened, and pressured to punish Jesus. The crowd called for Pilate to release Barabbas and crucify Jesus. The soldiers humiliated Jesus by stripping off his clothes and dividing them in four shares. Jesus's mother and the disciple whom Jesus loved boldly stood under the cross of Jesus. Joseph of Arimathea asked for the body of Jesus to give it a proper burial. The story of Jesus's passion and death is filled with people who are fickle, fraudulent, and faithful. As twenty-first-century believers, where do we see ourselves in the story?

Pray

Jesus,

The story of your arrest, crucifixion, and death reveals the true nature of your followers' hearts.

May your valiant fidelity in embracing the cross inspire us never to shirk from the challenges of being your disciples.

Amen.

Ponder

How have I betrayed Jesus in the past week?

EASTER VIGIL
(MATTHEW 28:1–10):

One and the Same

Matthew's version of Easter morning has a curious detail not found in the other Gospels. "Mary Magdalene and the other Mary" were rewarded for their faithful presence at Jesus's death, his burial, and now at his tomb. Jesus met these two women after they had been sent by an angel to announce Jesus's resurrection to his disciples (whom Jesus calls "my brothers," indicating his forgiveness after they had deserted him). This Jesus whom they encounter is not a ghost, a spirit, or a phantom. By having the two women embrace the feet of Jesus, Matthew is deliberately showing us that the Jesus who died on the cross is the same Jesus who has been raised from the dead.

Pray

Risen Jesus,
Your life did not end on Good Friday. It
continued Easter morning.

The two Marys' fidelity was rewarded
with an encounter with you.

The disciples' infidelity was forgiven.

May we live with the fidelity of the
two Marys and the knowledge of our
forgiveness when we run from you.

Amen.

Ponder

How do I experience the Risen Jesus?

THE EASTER SEASON

EASTER SUNDAY, MASS DURING THE DAY
(JOHN 20:1–9)

Death Is Dead

The Gospel of John is the only Gospel that tells us when Simon Peter arrived at the tomb and went in, he saw the burial cloths "and the cloth that had covered [Jesus's] head, not with the burial cloths but rolled up in a separate place." What are we to make of this curious detail about the rolled-up head covering? Scholars suggest an interesting interpretation. Unlike resuscitated Lazarus who came out of his tomb wrapped in his burial cloths and needed to be unbound, thus suggesting he is still subject to his humanity, the Risen Christ transcended our human existence with its burial cloths. Combined with the Greek grammatical construction, the rolled-up head covering points to God's ultimate and unqualified conquest of death.

Pray

Risen Christ,

In raising you from the dead, your Father deliberately and definitively broke the bonds of death and ushered in a new and unimaginable reality.

Our Baptism offers us hope of transcending death and living in this new reality.

Amen.

Ponder

What experiences have helped me to believe that death is not the end?

Probe My Wounds

She sobbed over her daughter's death by suicide. "I should have seen it coming. My faith in God is destroyed." I shared with her what I have learned after five decades of reflecting on my own father's suicide. I told her that many people experience guilt for being blind to possible warning signs. I mentioned how it's hard to believe that God judges with the quickness of a human heart—"I don't think God judges an entire life based upon a final act of desperation." And I said the wound will always remain, but it does stop bleeding. In today's Gospel, the Risen Christ still has his wounds, and in probing them, Thomas, like this woman listening to me, found the faith to call Jesus "My Lord and My God!"

SECOND SUNDAY OF EASTER

Pray

Risen Christ,
Like yours, the wounds of our hearts
remain—but some no longer bleed.

May we never hesitate to allow others
to probe them so they might come to
deeper faith in you.

Amen.

Ponder

When have others probed my wounds
and rediscovered faith and hope?

The "Journey" of the Eucharist

The story of the two disciples encountering the Risen Christ as they journey to Emmaus is unique to Luke. It consists of five important movements. First, the Risen Jesus joins Cleopas and another disciple on their journey but they do not recognize him. Second, having been told of the events that occurred in Jerusalem over the past few days, Jesus explains the Scriptures that refer to the Messiah suffering and so entering into his glory. Third, at table, Jesus takes, blesses, and breaks bread and then shares it with the two. Fourth, the two disciples recognize who their companion is while he vanishes from their sight. They go on mission to announce their discovery. This story has strong Eucharistic overtones as we gather together, have

Scripture read and explained, share blessed bread, recognize the continuing presence of the Risen Christ in our midst, and are sent.

———

Pray

Risen Jesus,
In the celebration of the Eucharist, we recognize your continuing presence and our mission.
May our hearts burn within us.
Amen.

Ponder

How does the Eucharist challenge me?

A Different Kind of Shepherd

The imagery of today's Gospel comes straight from the pastoral life of first-century Palestine. Shepherds were notorious for stealing the sheep of others—the "thieves and robbers" mentioned by Jesus—and therefore were considered sinners. Jesus no doubt shocked his listeners by sanitizing the image and applying it to himself. He is a different kind of shepherd who is so invested in his sheep that he has given each a name. And the sheep are so trusting of the shepherd that they confidently respond to the shepherd's call and follow him. And where are they led? Not only to pasture, but more importantly, to life in abundance.

Pray

Loving Jesus,
You are the good shepherd who is so invested in us that you give each of us a name.

Open our ears to hear your call amid the clamor of our lives.

Open our hearts to follow you with confidence without straying from the fold.

Open our lives to experience abundant life.

Amen.

Ponder

How do I experience the life in abundance that Jesus offers?

Until We Meet Again

Today's Gospel is bittersweet as Jesus bids farewell to his disciples. He encourages them not to be troubled by his absence because it will only be temporary. He is returning to his Father to prepare a dwelling place for them and then will return to bring them to his Father's house. By proclaiming himself as "the way and the truth and the life," Jesus is giving his disciples a task to do as they wait for his return. By walking his way, believing the truth of his teaching, and experiencing the life they receive through discipleship, they can continue his ministry and do the works that he did—and even "greater ones"! Even in his apparent absence Christ is present through the life and ministry of his followers.

Pray

Risen Christ,

You are forever with us as we gather in your name and celebrate in Word and Sacrament.

May we continue your ministry among us through fidelity to your way, your truth, and your life.

Amen.

Ponder

How do I bring Christ's presence to others?

A God Who Sticks Around

It's so easy to feel abandoned when we lose a mentor, a teacher, a parent, or a trusted friend. We feel the loss even though their teachings and example live on in our memories. Anticipating their feeling of abandonment, Jesus promises the disciples, "I will not leave you orphans." He will ask the Father who will give us "another Advocate." The Greek word for Advocate also means "helper" or "mediator." Jesus was our first advocate, helper, and mediator. The Spirit of truth is our second and will be with us and in us always. Unlike our mentors, teachers, parents, and friends, this gift of the Spirit witnesses to the permanent, real presence and continuing care of God in our midst. God is determined never to let us feel forgotten or forsaken.

Pray

Ever-present God,
You never leave us stranded or deserted.

Through the gift and action of the Spirit, you continue to be present to us.

May we always live with the awareness of this reality.

Amen.

Ponder

How have I experienced the continuing presence and indwelling of the Spirit?

Mission Accomplished

I have done what was mine to do. I'm ready to go home and be with God." And with that, Veronica closed her eyes and breathed her last. In the face of death, rather than being filled with regrets for missed opportunities, rattled with fear, or begging for forgiveness, Veronica had the sense that her life's mission had been completed. Consequently, she was blessed with a peaceful death. Jesus expresses the same sentiment to the Father in today's Gospel: "Father, the hour has come. . . . I glorified you on earth by accomplishing the work that you gave me to do." Like Veronica and Jesus, we all are challenged to glorify God by discovering and fulfilling our life's mission.

Pray

Jesus,

You announced the kingdom of God to
all who would listen and showed them
how to live in it.

In doing so, you glorified your Father.

May we too give glory to the Father by
faithfully doing what we have been called
to do.

Amen.

Ponder

How will I feel about my life when death
approaches?

THE ASCENSION OF THE LORD
(MATTHEW 28:16–20)

A Stunted Disciple?

On this feast of the Ascension, we read the conclusion of Matthew's Gospel. The disciples arrive at a Galilean mountaintop where they encounter and worship Jesus. In this Gospel, however, Jesus does not ascend into heaven. He commissions his disciples to do four things: to go out, to make disciples of the nations, to baptize, and to teach. Jesus will be with them "until the end of the age" as they fulfill this commission. Indeed, the next chapter of the Gospel will be written by the lives of his disciples. And that includes us. A contemporary disciple without a sense of mission is a stunted disciple.

THE ASCENSION OF THE LORD

Pray

Risen Christ,

Like the eleven disciples, you send us on mission to announce the good news of the kingdom, to baptize, and to teach.

When we are weary or discouraged, help us to remember that you are always with us.

May the mission the Father entrusted you with bear fruit in our lives.

Amen.

Ponder

How does a sense of mission energize my Christian discipleship?

What's Your Wind, Rudder, and Compass?

On Pentecost, we celebrate God's gift of himself in the person of the Holy Spirit. The very words *spirit*uality and *spirit*ual life, suggest the preeminence of this gift in our lives. The Holy Spirit is the wind, the rudder, and the compass for our journey. It's because of the Spirit that we can die to ourselves, do charitable deeds, forgive our neighbor, and become people of prayer. No wonder Saint Paul reminds us in the Letter to the Galatians to "live . . . and be guided by the Spirit" (5:25). Without the Spirit, we drift aimlessly on the sea of life.

Pray

Come, Holy Spirit,
Open the doors of our hearts and fill us
with your presence.

Give us the wisdom to know how to
act.

Grant us the sensitivity to follow your
slightest promptings that push us beyond
our selfishness and sin.

With your holy counsel and heavenly
direction, we can discover and explore
the harbor of freedom where your selfless
saints abide.

Amen.

Ponder

How do I live guided by the Spirit?

ORDINARY TIME

THE MOST HOLY TRINITY
(JOHN 3:16–18)

Dance Your Life Away

One of the first mysteries we learn as children is that God is a Trinity: The Father is a father because he has a son. The Son is a son because he has a father. And this relationship is bonded together by the gift of the Holy Spirit. One God, three Persons. At the very heart of God is a dynamic trinitarian dance of love. Because we are created "in the image and likeness of God," we too are called to a dynamic dance of love in our lives: love God, love our neighbor, and love ourselves. This trinity in our lives reflects the divine Trinity.

THE MOST HOLY TRINITY

Pray

Blessed Trinity, Father, Son, and Holy
Spirit,

You are a dynamic dance of love
that shapes, supports, and sustains all
relationships.

Teach us the steps so we might enter
your divine dance.

May our delight in the dance be
displayed in our decision to love you,
others, and ourselves.

Let us dance our lives away with love.

Amen.

Ponder

How can I express my love for God,
others, and myself today?

THE MOST HOLY BODY AND BLOOD OF CHRIST
(JOHN 6:51–58)

Become What You Receive

The Eucharist is a vivid reminder of the ministry of Jesus. He spent his life breaking his body and pouring out his blood for the needs of people and the salvation of the world. The Eucharist is also his real, continuing presence in our midst. When we receive the Eucharist, we become united to Jesus's ministry and person as we discover our truest identity as the Bread of Life and Body of Christ on earth. Our "Amen" at communion time not only acknowledges the true presence of Jesus in the Eucharist but also affirms our mission to lovingly sacrifice our lives for others and the world.

Pray

Lord Jesus,

You are truly present in the Eucharist.

In your body and blood, you show us the essence of selfless love.

In our reception of the Eucharist, you challenge us with knowledge of our truest identity.

Grant us the grace to be faithful to our vocation of being the Bread of Life for the world.

Amen.

Ponder

How can I be the Bread of Life for someone today?

SECOND SUNDAY IN ORDINARY TIME
(JOHN 1:29–34)

Instant Recognition

John proclaims Jesus as "the Lamb of God, who takes away the sin of the world." The scriptural references would not have been lost on John's listeners. It hints to the Passover, the rite celebrating Israel's liberation from Egyptian slavery, when the lamb's blood marked and protected the homes of the Israelites. It also is reminiscent of Isaiah's suffering servant, who is led like a lamb to the slaughter as a sin-offering. Saint Paul will pick up on this image in his First Letter to the Corinthians, as does the Book of Revelation. And at every celebration of the Eucharist, before communion, we repeat this ancient title and insight of John the Baptist.

SECOND SUNDAY IN ORDINARY TIME

Pray

Lord Jesus,

In your great love, you give us yourself as food for the journey.

You come to us to free us from our slavery to sin.

Lamb of God, you take away the sin of the world, have mercy on us.

Amen.

Ponder

What meaning do I find in calling Jesus "the Lamb of God, who takes away the sin of the world"?

Change Your Thinking

"Clean up your act! God is taking over!" That's how a college student paraphrased Jesus's initial proclamation in today's Gospel, "Repent, for the kingdom of heaven is at hand." Unfortunately, the student missed the mark. The Greek word *metanoia* in its basic meaning does not connote a moral conversion, a turning from sin, or an amendment of life. Rather, it connotes a fundamental change in thinking and living. "Kingdom" refers to "kingly rule" or "reign," and not a geographical territory. Perhaps a better paraphrase of Jesus's statement would be, "Change the way you think about everything! Divine grace is starting its influence!"

THIRD SUNDAY IN ORDINARY TIME

Pray

Jesus,
You proclaimed to us a new reality where God's favor and kindness would be at work in our lives.

This requires us to radically change the way we think about ourselves and our neighbors—and even those we call the enemy.

May your ministry transform our thoughts and lead us to live in the abundant grace of God.

Amen.

Ponder

How do Jesus's teachings and actions challenge my thinking?

FOURTH SUNDAY IN ORDINARY TIME
(MATTHEW 5:1–12A)

An Incisive Critique

Far from an airy-fairy, pious teaching, the Beatitudes are an incisive critique of the values and codes of behavior found in the twenty-first century. In a world where success is measured by possessions, Jesus called blessed those who are poor in spirit. In a country where pain and death are avoided at all costs, Jesus called blessed those who mourn. In companies and corporations where people jockey for power, Jesus called blessed those who are meek. In a litigious society that often seeks revenge, Jesus called blessed peacemakers and the merciful. Though Jesus taught the Beatitudes two thousand years ago, they remain timeless challenges and critiques of our contemporary culture.

FOURTH SUNDAY IN ORDINARY TIME

Pray

Jesus,
Your Beatitudes turn the standards and
ethics of our world topsy-turvy.

They reveal to us that in the kingdom
of heaven, there's more to life than meets
the eye.

Give us the grace to embrace these
counter-cultural teachings and to live
them out at home and in the office.

May we come to be called "blessed."
Amen.

Ponder

How do the Beatitudes challenge my
current way of living?

FIFTH SUNDAY IN ORDINARY TIME
(MATTHEW 5:13–16)

For the Sake of Others

The disciples are called "the salt of the earth" and "the light of the world." Consequently, their success will rest on not drawing attention to themselves. As salt is used for preservation and purification, the disciples are called to preserve what is good and purify what hinders God's reign. They cannot allow themselves to become "tasteless salt" that is diluted or dissolved by the cares and worries of the world. As light moves beyond itself and illumines objects in a room, the disciples are called to look beyond themselves by doing good works. This will lead others to glorify God, whom Matthew, for the first time, refers to as "your heavenly Father."

FIFTH SUNDAY IN ORDINARY TIME

Pray

Lord of all creation,
You call us to be salt and light.

As salt, we are called to draw out and enhance your Father's love in the world.

As light, we are called to live for the sake of others.

As salt and light, may we never draw attention to ourselves.

Amen.

Ponder

How can I live out my vocation as salt and light?

A New Interpretation

I have come not to abolish [the Law] but to fulfill." Jesus is an observant Jew, devoted not to break or replace the Law, but to interpret it for a new situation, namely, the incoming of God's reign. In four antithetical statements, each of which begins with "You have heard that it was said . . . :," followed by a command, "But I say to you . . .," Jesus declares the former interpretation of the Law inadequate and replaces it with a more rigorous interpretation. His interpretation addresses interior attitudes and motivations of the heart that often lead to behaviors that violate the Law. Notice how his interpretation focuses on right relationships among people.

SIXTH SUNDAY IN ORDINARY TIME

Pray

Jesus,

You brought a new understanding of our covenant with your Father.

Your teaching challenges us to look beneath our external obedience to the Law and to focus on the interior attitudes of our hearts.

Those interior attitudes reveal the quality of our relationships with others.

Amen.

Ponder

What do the attitudes of my heart tell me about the quality of my relationships?

SEVENTH SUNDAY IN ORDINARY TIME
(MATTHEW 5:38–48)

Just Say No!

Is Jesus asking us to be a doormat by teaching us to "offer no resistance to one who is evil"? No. He is teaching us a spiritual truth about renouncing our reactive instincts and responding with nonviolence and nonretaliation. Physical violence, an unjust lawsuit, forced labor, or indebtedness due to an inconvenient borrower can backfire on our aggressor; a nonviolent response might cause the person to be ashamed and perhaps even move the person to repentance. Nonviolence and nonretaliation can transform the heart, making us children of the Father who love, treat, and pray for friend or foe equally. This is what it means to be "perfect as your heavenly Father"—not in moral perfection but in spiritual maturity.

SEVENTH SUNDAY IN ORDINARY TIME

Pray
Jesus,
You call us to stop the cycle of violence and injustice, absorb their energy, and transform them into an instrument of peace and generosity.

In doing this, we not only show our adoption as children of your Father but also our spiritual maturity.

May we never return insult for insult or injury for injury.

Amen.

Ponder
What is my usual response to insult, injury, and injustice?

Become God's Agent

It's so easy to worry, fret, and become anxious about the necessities of daily life. In one of the most beloved teachings of Jesus, our attention is directed to nature, specifically, the birds in the sky and wildflowers. Jesus uses them as an example of God's care and concern *for us*: as God feeds the birds who do not work for their food and clothes the flowers in royal splendor surpassing that of Solomon, so too God provides for all that we need. God's help and solicitude are expressed through the disciples who, making God's reign and right relations with others a priority, respond to those in need. Worry is an insult to God as long as there are faithful disciples of Jesus.

Pray

God of all creation,
Your care and consideration for us are often expressed through your children whose charity and generosity help to alleviate the challenges and difficulties that others face.

May we always serve you by being attentive to the needs of others.

Amen.

Ponder

How am I an instrument of God's care and concern for others?

Rock or Sand?

Some people judge a person's faith and holiness through one's intellectual assent: proclaiming Jesus as Lord and Savior; believing in the Real Presence in the Eucharist. Other people judge a person's faith and holiness by charismatic gifts (prophecy, exorcism, miracle working). Jesus rejects both ideas. For him, holiness and alignment with God's will are about listening to his teaching and acting on them. Jesus's words must lead to a believer's work. Such a response provides a rock foundation that can survive life's emotional storms, tornadoes, and hurricanes. To just listen to his words and not act on them is to be "like a fool who built his house on sand."

Pray

Jesus,

You are the wise teacher whose words have a dynamism that must find expression. They are meant not only to inform but also to transform how we live in this world.

By letting your words shape how we live, we build on bedrock that offers safety and security in trying times.

Amen.

Ponder

What areas of my life are built on sand? On rock?

Come to the Table!

Gentiles and Jews who did not keep the Law either because of immorality or their profession (tax collectors, shepherds, prostitutes, wool dyers) were called "sinners." Such people would not be found sharing a meal with observant Jews since meals were rituals of friendship and intimacy. Jesus violated this social convention by eating with Matthew the tax collector and other sinners. When challenged on his behavior, Jesus cited a saying from the prophet Hosea that highlights the importance of mercy over sacrifice and indicated that his mission was to sinners and not the righteous. Jesus's action and teaching challenged the self-righteous smugness of those who considered themselves holier-than-thou.

Pray

Jesus,

Despite our faults, weaknesses, and sins, you invite us to your table.

You are not embarrassed or ashamed to be seen in our company, for it is precisely for us sinners that your Father sent you.

May your mercy and the food and nourishment you provide give us the strength to follow you more closely.

Amen.

Ponder

Where has self-righteous smugness crept into my life?

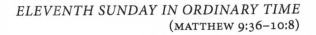

Gracefully Called and Sinfully Sent

One can only wonder what Jesus saw in the motley group of twelve disciples whom he chose as his apostles. Simon Peter, nicknamed the "Rock," was a bit fickle and denied Jesus three times to save his own skin. James and John, the sons of Zebedee, wanted to share in Jesus's glory without any pain or suffering. Matthew, the former tax collector, had been a collaborator with the Romans. Judas Iscariot betrayed Jesus for thirty pieces of silver. So why this ragtag group of misfits? Perhaps to show that God calls the questionable and qualifies them with divine grace.

Pray

Jesus,
You chose questionable misfits as
apostles and commissioned them
not only to proclaim the kingdom of
heaven but also to perform healings and
exorcisms in your name.

In the same way, you call us, despite
our failings and sins, to witness to your
kingdom.

May we always live with the conscious
awareness that your grace, and your
grace alone, qualifies us to minister in
your name.

Amen.

Ponder

How am I called to minister for the
kingdom?

TWELFTH SUNDAY IN ORDINARY TIME
(MATTHEW 10:26–33)

Shout It!

Jesus instructs the apostles to preach with boldness, courage, and conviction—"speak in the light . . . proclaim on the housetops." The message of the kingdom is for everyone. Knowing full well that the message might rattle some cages and find resistance, three times in today's Gospel Jesus cautions his apostles not to be afraid. Those who oppose the message of the kingdom can only take one's physical life, not one's eternal life. Just as the Father watches over the sparrows that are sold for next to nothing, so too the Father's investment in the apostles is seen in knowing the number of strands of hair on an apostle's head. Unwavering proclamation of the kingdom of heaven is met with the abiding protection of God.

Pray

Jesus,

You send us on mission to enthusiastically proclaim your Father's unconditional love and forgiveness.

Such a declaration of divine devotion might be opposed.

May we fearlessly face that opposition knowing you are watching over us.

Amen.

Ponder

How do I boldly and courageously proclaim the message of the kingdom of heaven?

The Challenge of the Mission

Today's Gospel concludes Jesus's commissioning of his apostles. The Divine Master makes clear that the mission he entrusts to his followers gives their lives their ultimate meaning. That is why it supersedes their attachment to what they dearly love, namely, their families and their very lives. This mission will involve sacrifices and persecutions—"the cross"—just as it did in the life of Jesus. Acceptance of these mission-centered sufferings is one way disciples show they are serious about following in the footprints of the Master; so do their reception of and hospitality toward other disciples.

THIRTEENTH SUNDAY IN ORDINARY TIME

Pray

Divine Master,
You did not skirt or sugarcoat the requirements and demands our mission entails.

You forthrightly laid them out before us and encouraged us to accept them.

In doing so, you highlighted the mission as the priority and ultimate meaning of our lives.

May we follow in your footprints by embracing our crosses and offering loving acceptance to everyone we encounter on the way.

Amen.

Ponder

What are some of the challenging consequences of my Christian discipleship?

The Yoke of Love

The second half of today's Gospel is an often-misunderstood saying of Jesus. Jesus is talking about the Jewish Law and our relationship to it. Over the years, the Pharisees began to refer to the Mosaic Law as the "yoke of the Law" and believed that through strict obedience to it, they could offer God their devotion. As they embellished the Law, it became a heavy burden that weighed down pious Jews. Like a poorly made yoke for two oxen, it rubbed against and chafed the heart. Jesus's yoke—his interpretation of the Law—is easy because he takes the lead with love. His example of meekness and humility moves us beyond legalism as we work the field for justice and mercy. In that field we offer God our worship and find refreshment for the tasks ahead.

Pray

Jesus,

You free us from strict legalism by calling us to love God, ourselves, and others.

May this love free our heavy hearts and lead us to true devotion to your Father.

Amen.

Ponder

How do Jesus's teachings unburden me?

A Sower's Sown Seed

Today's parable includes the sower, the seed, the soil, and the harvest. Focusing on each renders a different dimension of this parable. The sower's prodigal and indiscriminate sowing of the seed on every kind of soil, regardless of its condition, highlights a universal invitation to everyone. Emphasizing the seed (which represents the word of the kingdom) reveals its ability to accomplish its purpose even though much falls on questionable soil. Attention to the soil underlines the attitudes and conditions necessary for the seed to germinate and come to fruition. The harvest of fruit—"a hundred or sixty or thirtyfold"—is staggering considering a good harvest yielded tenfold; God's reign will far exceed what we could ever imagine.

Pray

God,
You generously call every one of us into your kingdom.

Your scattered seed will indeed accomplish the purpose for which you sent it even though it might not be nourished by all who receive it.

May the soil of our hearts be rich and receptive, yielding your bountiful harvest.

Amen.

Ponder

Which dimension of the parable of the sower strikes me?

Something's Cooking!

Today's Gospel is optimistic. The parable of the weeds among the wheat reminds us not to become discouraged. God is very much in charge and in the end, he will rid the world of evil. In the parable of the mustard seed, Jesus teaches that the kingdom of heaven is not an immense sequoia tree transplanted in our midst. Rather, it starts like a simple herb growing in our own backyard—a pat on the back, a kind word, an apology, a handwritten sympathy note—that catches the attention of others, hinting to God's inclusive love for all. The final parable mentions a woman literally "hiding" yeast, often a biblical symbol of evil and corruption, in three measures of dough (about fifty pounds). It offers hope to those marginalized and excluded, witnessing to the transformative, life-giving power of God's reign.

Pray

God,
Your kingdom's fullness has mysteriously begun.

In the face of the evil in the world, grant us the grace to remain optimistic, knowing that something's cooking in our midst.

Amen.

Ponder

What keeps me optimistic?

Hidden and in Plain View

We hear three short parables about the kingdom of heaven today. In the first parable, a person unexpectedly finds a treasure in a field. The person buries it again, and then sells everything to buy the field. The surprise of the find elevates the person's joy. In the second, a merchant goes in search of fine pearls. He too is surprised by unwittingly discovering a pearl beyond his expectations—"of great price." He also sells all his possessions to buy that pearl. These two parables highlight that the kingdom of heaven will catch us off guard and be a joyful and surprising discovery. This discovery requires a response: the complete investment of oneself and one's resources. The third parable reminds us that the net of the kingdom will ultimately catch everyone, and the righteous will be separated from the wicked.

———

Pray

Loving God,
Your kingdom is both hidden and in plain view.

May our awareness and discovery of it lead to the endless joy of our total commitment.

Amen.

Ponder

When have I been surprised by God's kingdom?

EIGHTEENTH SUNDAY IN ORDINARY TIME
(MATTHEW 14:13–21)

More than Enough

Today's miracle of the feeding of the multitude has rich dimensions. It portrays a compassionate Jesus who is willing to satisfy the physical hunger of people, thus suggesting God's interest in our most basic needs. Surprisingly, God feeds us by using ordinary people as instruments of divine generosity. When we share what we have with others, there is always more than enough to go around because God miraculously makes up for what is lacking. The Eucharistic overtones are obvious as Jesus takes, blesses, breaks, and gives the bread to the disciples for distribution. The twelve wicker baskets of leftovers remind us how the twelve tribes of Israel will be reunited in the kingdom of heaven and, with all of us, enjoy the heavenly banquet.

Pray

Jesus,

You used the feeding of the multitude to teach us important lessons.

You make our meager provisions adequate to satisfy the most basic hungers of others when we are willing to share.

May our charity and generosity reflect your divine investment in our lives.

Amen.

Ponder

What am I unwilling to share with others?

Beyond Your Comfort Zone

Being obedient, the disciples follow Jesus's instructions to get into a boat and precede him to the other side of the lake. Their obedience leads them into the midst of a frightening storm. This reminds us that obedience to God's call does not always bring peace of mind with no emotional upheavals. Jesus appears walking on the stormy sea toward the disciples, indicating that Jesus does not take away the darkness and difficulties of life but, as he did with Peter, he calls us to move beyond our comfort zone and step forward in faith into a precarious situation. Peter miraculously and momentarily walks on water, and when his lack of confidence in God's grace causes him to sink, Jesus rescues him.

Pray

Jesus,
During challenging times, you come walking toward us.

We don't always recognize you—but you are always lovingly present to us.

As you call us out of our comfort zone, may we keep our eyes fixed on you.

May we never doubt your grace.

Amen.

Ponder

When did Jesus's call stretch me?

A Mother's Love

Some participants in a women's Bible study read today's Gospel through the lens of Pope Francis's advocacy for the further inclusion of women in the life of the Church. One participant, the mother of three children, brought a different understanding based upon her parental experience: "The Canaanite was a mother who was willing to do anything for the health of her daughter!" The Canaanite acknowledges Jesus as the Jewish Messiah—"Lord, Son of David!"—and pleads for an exorcism. Jesus is coldly silent. When pressed, Jesus acknowledges his mission is exclusively to the Jews. The woman pleads again. When Jesus insults her with an ethnic slur, the woman repeats the slur, cleverly turning the tables on Jesus. This mother's tenacity—what

Jesus calls "great faith"—broke the Jew-Gentile barrier in Jesus's mind and helped him reveal his inclusive mission to all people.

Pray

———

Jesus,

You did not turn down a foreign mother's unshakable and persistent love for her child.

May I have the same for the people for whom I am responsible.

Amen.

Ponder

How accepting am I of foreigners?

Rock-Solid Faith

Have you ever wondered what people say about you behind your back? Ever wonder what your family and friends really think of you? Though such musings can indicate an over investment in your reputation, they can also suggest interest in other people's insights into your self-understanding and identity. Perhaps it was that latter interest that motivated Jesus to ask today's two questions: "Who do people say that the Son of Man is?" "But who do you say that I am?" Peter's response, proclaimed in pagan territory, not only points to Jesus's messianic mission to all nations and peoples but also, playing on Peter's name, becomes the rock-solid foundation of the sacramental life of the Church.

Pray

Son of the living God,
Simon Peter was the first to proclaim you
the Messiah of all people.

That proclamation forms the
foundation of our faith and our Church.

May our lives be built on that
foundation and, in difficult times, become
the reason for our hope and trust.

Amen.

Ponder

Who do I say Jesus is?

Finding Your Life

Peter's supposedly rock-solid proclamation of Jesus as the Messiah in last week's Gospel might have been an impulsive declaration. It appears to crack as Peter hears about Jesus's future suffering and death and rebukes Jesus for accepting such a fate. The apostle clearly wants Jesus and the Messianic mission on his own terms. Jesus is uncompromising and rejects Peter's understanding as obstructing the will of God: "You are thinking not as God does, but as human beings do." Jesus makes clear that God's will not only demands our entire lives but also has consequences that will help us find the ultimate meaning to our existence—what Jesus calls "losing one's life for my sake in order to find it."

TWENTY-SECOND SUNDAY IN ORDINARY TIME

Pray

Jesus,

Your life and teaching challenge us not to cling to our understanding of what brings happiness and meaning to our lives.

Your Father's will challenges our feeble understanding of the kingdom of heaven.

Only by following your Father's will do we find the true meaning to life.

Amen.

Ponder

When have I questioned the will of God?

Steps to Reconciliation

Today's Gospel shows us how to deal with conflict between members of a Christian community. When someone sins against us, instead of gossiping about the sinner, we directly confront the sinner in hopes the person will make amends and we are reconciled. If the sinner refuses, we bring along one or two people as impartial witnesses to help win the sinner's repentance. If that fails, the community confronts the individual. If that is unsuccessful, then we treat the person "as you would a Gentile or a tax collector." It's unclear if such a statement means the sinner is excluded from the community or that the community should continue to accept and love the person as Jesus did with foreigners and public sinners. Forgiveness does not always lead to reconciliation between two people.

———

Pray

Merciful Jesus,
You call us to imitate you in our acceptance, mercy, and forgiveness of others.

When we are betrayed, we forgive and seek reconciliation.

May the lack of reconciliation never harden our hearts to others.

Amen.

Ponder

When have I refused to be reconciled with someone?

The Scales of Justice

Jesus responds to Peter's question about forgiving "seven times," seven being the perfect number and thus suggesting perfect forgiveness, with the exorbitant "seventy-seven times." His response clearly suggests that the refusal to forgive is never an option. Jesus buttresses his teaching with the parable of an unforgiving servant who, having a huge debt remitted by his master, subsequently refused to remit a far lesser debt owed to him by a fellow servant. The master punished the cold and cruel heartlessness of the unforgiving servant. God's forgiveness of our sins obliges and compels us to act in a similar way toward others. We ultimately set the terms of our own judgment by the measure of forgiveness and mercy we show others.

TWENTY-FOURTH SUNDAY IN ORDINARY TIME

Pray

Loving God of mercy and forgiveness,
You graciously erase the debt of our sins
without batting an eye.

You call us to imitate you by forgiving
those who sin against us.

May your forgiveness of our sins soften
our hearts toward others and motivate us
to show mercy.

Amen.

Ponder

Who have I not forgiven? Why?

Today's Gift of Grace

Day laborers stood on the lowest rung of the economic ladder and needed a day's wage to provide food for themselves and their families. Today's parable focuses on God's concern for our daily necessities and everyone's right—even those we deem unworthy—to have food for the day. But it's not just about how God helps us to put food on the table. It's also about God's generosity. How tempting it is to think that we can earn God's grace as payment for a daytime or lifetime of prayer, fasting, and alms giving. Grace is never deserved or earned. It is lavishly, liberally, and lovingly given by a God who knows exactly what we need for today and provides it.

TWENTY-FIFTH SUNDAY IN ORDINARY TIME

Pray

God of all grace,
You know our most basic daily needs,
both physical and spiritual, and never
hesitate to provide for them.

May we never presume we can force
your hand or earn your grace, gift, or
blessing.

May we never envy your kindness and
charity toward others.

Amen.

Ponder

What grace has God freely given me
today?

Spiritual Maturity

Today's parable and its interpretation are unique to Matthew. The first son shames his father by telling him directly he will not obey his request to work in the vineyard; later changing his mind, he went to work. The second son lied to his father but, in the end, did not go to work. In responding to Jesus's question, "Which of the two did his father's will?", the chief priests and elders condemn themselves. They appeared obedient like the second son, but ultimately resisted John's call to conversion. Tax collectors and prostitutes are likened to the first son; they initially said no to God but later responded to John's call to conversion. Consequently, they are entering the kingdom of God ahead of the religious authorities. Ideally our words should align with our actions, but when they don't, it is our actions that betray the depths of our spiritual maturity.

———

Pray

Lord Jesus,
May we never hesitate to positively respond to your call both in word and in deed.
    Amen.

Ponder

When have I been like the two sons?

Tending the Vineyard

Matthew interprets Jesus's parable as an allegory about salvation history. God is the landowner who has given the religious authorities the vineyard of the kingdom, and as its tenants, they are responsible for its produce. Instead of handing over the produce to the designated servants, the tenants treat the servants like the prophets of old and refuse to listen to them, responding to them with violence and murder. When God sends his son, the tenants seize and kill him as will happen to Jesus. When Jesus asks them how the landowner will respond to the tenants, the religious authorities condemn themselves by calling for the tenants' deaths and for the vineyard to be given to others who will produce the fruit at the proper time.

Matthew's point is that the kingdom of God is a gift given to people who will live according to its values.

———

Pray

Lord Jesus,
The gift of the kingdom requires a radical transformation in how we live.

May our thoughts, words, and actions make manifest its fruit.

Amen.

Ponder

How do I manifest the values of the kingdom?

A Dress Code for Eternity

Today's parable likens the kingdom of heaven proclaimed by Jesus to a joyful celebration of love, much like a wedding banquet held by a king for his son. When the invited guests refuse the invitation, some going so far as to prioritize their work and business over it, the king angrily responds and sends his servants with an invitation to the poorest people. Everyone—"bad and good alike"—is invited to it. The evangelist concludes with a detail not found in his sources. The king discovers a guest who is not dressed properly and throws him out of the banquet. The parable optimistically suggests the kingdom can be entered into here and now. But it does require repentance and conversion of life, symbolized by the appropriate wedding garment.

TWENTY-EIGHTH SUNDAY IN ORDINARY TIME

Pray

Jesus,

The kingdom of heaven you proclaimed is a joyful celebration of love that is already in our midst.

May our thoughts, words, and actions be an appropriate garment that shows our eagerness to accept your invitation.

Amen.

Ponder

Am I dressed appropriately for the kingdom of heaven?

TWENTY-NINTH SUNDAY IN ORDINARY TIME
(MATTHEW 22:15–21)

We Belong to God

When maliciously asked by the Pharisees' disciples (who opposed it) and the Herodians (who supported it) about the legality of the unpopular poll tax, Jesus tricked the Pharisees' disciples into producing the very coin used for it, thus exposing their hypocrisy. Jesus pointed to the emperor's image and inscription on the Roman coin and famously said, "Repay to Caesar what belongs to Caesar and to God what belongs to God." Traditionally, this has been understood as believers being good citizens of their country. But there is a more important teaching Jesus is giving. Where is the image of God? The divine image is imprinted on the heart of every single person. As a result, our entire lives belong to God and should be so ordered.

TWENTY-NINTH SUNDAY IN ORDINARY TIME

Pray

Loving Creator,
You have created us in your image and likeness.

You challenge us, as masterpieces of your creativity, to live in such a way as to give you praise and glory.

May we cherish the fact that we belong to you.

Amen.

Ponder

How do I reflect the image and likeness of God?

The Two Loves

Though devout Jews considered all the Law of equal importance, there was interest in trying to sum it up in a simple statement. Jesus's response was to quote the *Shema*, "You shall love the Lord, your God, with all your heart, with all your soul, and with all your mind," prayed twice a day, as the "first and greatest commandment." The second commandment, love of neighbor, is taken from the Book of Leviticus. Love is the essence of Jesus's interpretation of the Law. To love God without love of neighbor is to have an otherworldly spirituality that has no practical implications for daily life. To love one's neighbor without love of God is to become a philanthropist with merely good intentions. From Jesus's perspective, one love compels the other love.

Pray

Jesus,
You set the example for love of God and
neighbor.

May our love for God push us into the
arms of our neighbors.

May our love of neighbor deepen our
love for your Father.

Amen.

Ponder

Where do I fail in my love of God and
neighbor?

Pride and Humility

In today's Gospel, Jesus criticizes the religious leaders who were learned in Torah ("scribes") and the lay religious leaders who interpreted the Law ("Pharisees"). He highlights their hypocrisy and lack of integrity (their actions do not match their words); their strict and burdensome interpretation of the Law that they lay on others; and their love for the attention they receive from showy religious practices, for the respect they receive in the marketplace and in the synagogue, and for titles. All these traits point to pride and self-exaltation. Jesus states a very different approach for those who follow him: "The greatest among you must be your servant. Whoever exalts himself will be humbled, but whoever humbles himself will be exalted."

THIRTY-FIRST SUNDAY OF ORDINARY TIME

Pray

Jesus,

As Master and Messiah, you walked the path of humility and opened your heart in service to all.

May we follow your example.

May our humility and willingness to serve be evidence of our discipleship.

Amen.

Ponder

In what areas of my spiritual life do I follow the scribes and Pharisees?

Be Prepared!

Today's parable is an allegory for the Christian community as we wait for the Son of Man. The kingdom of heaven is like a wedding banquet. It's an event of joy, not fear. Sadly, not all of us are fully prepared. Five virgins have brought oil (good works), five have not. When Christ the bridegroom was delayed, the ten virgins fell asleep, but they were not criticized for that. When the bridegroom did arrive, the wise virgins were unable to share their oil (good works) with the foolish virgins. They are not being selfish; rather, each person is responsible for how they have lived. When the bridegroom arrived, the wise virgins entered the banquet. The foolish virgins were locked out: saying "Lord, Lord" must be buttressed with good actions. Though the moral encourages us to stay awake, the parable is more about always being prepared.

———

Pray
Jesus,
Your Second Coming will be an occasion of gladness and great pleasure.

May we be prepared with the oil of peace, love, and justice.

Amen.

Ponder
How much oil do I have?

Stop Being Greedy!

Don't limit the interpretation of today's parable to using God-given gifts to the full. A master prepared for a journey by entrusting three servants, each according to his abilities, with a large sum of money ("talent"). The servants were expected to trade the talents and increase the master's wealth. In Jesus's day, people believed that wealth was limited so someone became rich at the expense of others. Rich people were seen as greedy and wicked. From this perspective, it was the third servant, who was cursed by his master, who did the ethical deed. Acknowledging the corruption of the master, "harvesting where [he] did not plant and gathering where [he] did not scatter"—an accusation the master did not deny—the servant stopped the cycle of greed and corruption. The parable calls for the rich to stop exploiting the poor and for the poor to expose the sin of greed.

———

Pray

Jesus,

You taught that the poor are blessed and possess the kingdom of heaven.

Transform our greed into generosity.
Amen.

Ponder

How do I exploit poor people?

Respond to the Need
in Front of You

Today's Gospel celebrates the works of mercy: feeding the hungry, giving drink to the thirsty, welcoming the stranger, clothing the naked, caring for the sick, and visiting the imprisoned. Since the Son of Man identifies with the hungry, thirsty, stranger, naked, sick, and prisoner, we are often told to "see Christ in the poor." But the sheep's surprise in discovering that they were ministering to the Son of Man without knowing it, reveals another important dimension to this parable. Unlike many of us who sleepwalk through the day and are blind to those in need, the sheep were living in the present moment and responding to the need in front of them.

Without their even knowing it, their response was an encounter with the divine: "Whatever you did for one of the least of mine, you did for me."

———

Pray

Jesus,

You remind us that those in need are a sacrament of your presence.

May we spontaneously respond to the unmet need before us.

Amen.

Ponder

How often do I sleepwalk through the day and am blind to the needy?

SOLEMNITIES and SPECIAL FEASTS

JANUARY 1
MARY, MOTHER OF GOD
(LUKE 2:16–21)

Mothering the Word

Today's Gospel presents Mary as a contemplative, keeping the words she heard about her son and "reflecting on them in her heart." She is not content, however, simply to pause, ponder, and pray. As today's solemnity reminds us, she had given birth to the Word of God. Saint Francis of Assisi challenges us to do the same. He writes, "We are mothers when we carry Him in our heart and body through a divine love and a pure and sincere conscience and give birth to Him through a holy activity which must shine as an example before others."

Pray

Blessed Mother,

We are called to follow your example and give birth to the Word of God by the way we live our lives.

Give us the inspiration and courage to do that among our family, friends, and coworkers.

Holy Mary, Mother of God, pray for us, sinners, now and at the hour of our death.

Amen.

Ponder

How can I become the mother of the Word of God during this new year?

Something's Lost that Must Be Found!

Ever wonder why we pray to Saint Anthony of Padua for help in finding lost or stolen things? Tradition says Anthony had a book of psalms that contained his teaching notes for use in the classroom. A young friar who had chosen to leave the Franciscans had taken the psalter with him. This book was hand-copied, and thus, an item of high value; a friar, given his vow of poverty, would have found such an item difficult to replace. Anthony prayed the book would be found or returned. The thief was moved not only to return the book but also to return to the Order. The story speaks eloquently of God's investment in the minutiae of our lives.

SAINT ANTHONY OF PADUA

Pray

Creator of the Universe,
Through the intercession of Saint
Anthony, you show your abiding concern
for us.

Your loving care pervades and
permeates the smallest details of our
lives.

May we always remember your
personal investment in us.

May we never hesitate to ask for your
help.

Amen.

Ponder

How has God revealed divine care and
concern for me?

What Wondrous Love!

Jesus is often portrayed with one hand pointing to his flaming heart and the other upraised. We could easily misinterpret this feast as a celebration of a part of Jesus's anatomy. It is so much more than that. Today, we celebrate Jesus's invitation to enter his heart and experience a wondrous love that surpasses all our hopes and desires. The fact that we have this feast dedicated to the Sacred Heart is a vivid reminder that most of us just can't wrap our heads around God's unconditional love. We betray it with conditions and try to earn it with our actions. As we respond to Jesus's invitation, let us never forget that God loves us unconditionally not because we are good but because God is good.

THE MOST SACRED HEART OF JESUS

Pray

Jesus,

Your sacred heart is ablaze with love and affection for us.

It illumines our lives, often darkened by guilty consciences and sinful actions.

May we always respond to the unconditional and limitless love you have for us.

Amen.

Ponder

When have I had glimmers and glimpses of God's unconditional love for me?

AUGUST 6
THE TRANSFIGURATION OF THE LORD
(SEE SECOND SUNDAY OF LENT)

AUGUST 11
SAINT CLARE OF ASSISI
(MATTHEW 19:27–29)

What Do You See in the Mirror?

In a letter to Blessed Agnes of Prague, Saint Clare of Assisi referred to the body of Jesus on the cross as a mirror. That's a surprising image. In meditating on the crucifix, Clare not only discovered the blessed poverty, holy humility, and ineffable charity of Jesus—but she also "saw" herself and how she was called to live! In this mystical mirror, Jesus revealed the secret to holiness: live simply, be humble, and above all, love. We do well to follow in those footprints.

SAINT CLARE OF ASSISI

Pray

Poor, humble, and loving Jesus,
You are a mirror that reveals to us the
secret to happiness and holiness.

You call us to live with the
outstretched hands of a beggar.

You challenge us to surrender our ego
and die to our pride.

And most of all, you command us to
stretch the size of our hearts in love and
acceptance of others.

May we come to see ourselves
mirrored in your final act of poverty,
humility, and love.

Amen.

Ponder

How do I see myself in the crucifix?

Gift, Grace, and Blessing

In today's Gospel, Mary sings of God's gift, grace, and blessing. Her being is a gift from God and is awash in grace. She is a vessel of God-given blessings and gratitude. She celebrates divine mercy and compassion that lift up the poor and lowly. She proclaims how God feeds the hungry and has been of help to her ancestors. Mary is acutely attentive to the reality of God's gift, grace, and blessing. At the end of her earthly life, she receives another grace and blessing by being the first to share in her Son's resurrection with the assumption of her body and soul into heaven. The divine gift that Mary enjoyed foreshadows the gift of the resurrection that will be given to us.

THE ASSUMPTION OF THE BLESSED VIRGIN MARY

Pray

Blessed Mary,

You were a faithful disciple of your Son.

Your fidelity was acknowledged and blessed by God who took you, body and soul, to share in eternal life.

May the hope of our own resurrection fuel our daily lives.

Amen.

Ponder

How does hope in the resurrection affect my thoughts, words, and actions?

God Provides

When most people think of Saint Francis, they think of a poor man. And indeed, he was poor. But his poverty was not a self-inflicted denial of material possessions and daily necessities. Rather, his poverty was first and foremost a radical act of trust in God. God was the alms giver who gave the saint everything he needed. Toward the end of his life as he looked over his forty-four years, Francis celebrated how God had graced him with his vocation, with brothers, with faith, and with a life of prayer. His poverty was proof positive that God can be trusted to provide abundantly.

SAINT FRANCIS OF ASSISI

Pray

Generous God,

You are the source of everything in our lives—our family, our friends, our clothes, the roof over our heads, and the meal set before us.

In your presence, we can claim nothing as our own, except for our sin.

Give us a radical trust in your divine guidance and care.

May we never insult you with our worries.

Amen.

Ponder

How has God provided for my needs?

It Takes All Types

Paul was a persecutor turned proclaimer of Christ. Antony of Egypt lived as a hermit. Martin of Tours was a soldier. Clare of Assisi renounced the wealth of her upbringing. Thomas Aquinas was a scholar. Julia Greeley was a former slave who generously shared what she had with people as poor as herself. Damien de Veuster and Marianne Cope ministered to Hansen's Disease patients in Hawaii. Emil Kapaun was a chaplain in the US Army. Carlo Acutis was a millennial who designed a website exploring Eucharistic miracles around the world. Gianna Beretta Molla was a pediatrician who refused both an abortion and a hysterectomy during a dangerous pregnancy. Today we celebrate the men and women who, each in their own unique way, lived the Beatitudes and are offered to us as role models. No matter our occupation, role, or position, we all are called to holiness.

———

Pray
Lord Jesus,
You proclaimed the Beatitudes as a blueprint for holiness.
May we live them in our own lives.
Amen.

Ponder
What's my unique path to holiness?

Full of Grace

Ever wonder what it would be like to live in a world without sin? Today's feast and Gospel give us a rare glimpse into that. Both celebrate and commemorate this singular gift given by God to a young virgin. Conceived and born untouched by the effects of sin, holy and without blemish, Mary is proclaimed by the archangel Gabriel as "full of grace." The very moment of her conception sings of the dignity of the human condition as a worthy womb for God. No wonder Saint Francis of Assisi calls Mary God's "Palace, Tabernacle, Dwelling, Robe, Servant, and Mother."

Pray

Blessed Mary,

By a rare grace from God, you were preserved from the effects of Adam and Eve's original sin.

And yet, this gift did not take away your freedom. You still freely proclaimed your "yes" to the invitation to become God's palace and tabernacle.

Though we experience the effects of sin in our own lives, may we have the courage to respond to every invitation from God.

Amen.

Ponder

What would my life look like without sin?

DECEMBER 12
OUR LADY OF GUADALUPE
(LUKE 1:26–38 OR 1:39–47)

The Mantle of Divine Love

On December 9, 1531, fifty-seven-year-old Juan Diego met a young pregnant mestiza, a woman of Amerindian and European heritage, dressed in the royal clothes of an Aztec goddess. With Elizabeth, he could have asked, "And how does this happen to me, that the mother of my Lord should come to me?" Though the widower's native land had been conquered recently by Spanish-speaking foreigners, the mestiza spoke to him in his native Nahuatl. That gives us an insight into the answer to Elizabeth's question, Mary's pregnancy, and today's feast: Christ was to be born not only in the Middle East but also in every land and every culture. Indeed, the mantle of God's love covers the entire earth.

OUR LADY OF GUADALUPE

Pray

Our Lady of Guadalupe,
In appearing to Juan Diego and speaking
in his native language, you have revealed
God's love for every culture on earth.

May your Son's grace expand the size
of our hearts so we can love and respect
every race, people, and culture.

Amen.

Ponder

What race, people, or culture do I look
upon with suspicion?

ABOUT THE AUTHOR

Ordained a Franciscan priest in 1983, Albert Haase, OFM, is a popular preacher and teacher. A former missionary to mainland China for over eleven years, he is the award-winning author of thirteen books on popular spirituality and the presenter on five bestselling DVDs. He currently resides in San Antonio TX. Visit his website at www.AlbertOFM.org

ABOUT THE PARACLETE PRESS

PARACLETE PRESS is the publishing arm of the Cape Cod Benedictine community, the Community of Jesus. Presenting a full expression of Christian belief and practice, we reflect the ecumenical charism of the Community and its dedication to sacred music, the fine arts, and the written word.

Learn more about us at our website:
www.paracletepress.com

ALBERT HAASE, OFM

CATCHING
FIRE
BECOMING
FLAME

A GUIDE FOR SPIRITUAL
TRANSFORMATION

www.paracletepress.com